HOW TO INVEST IN REAL ESTATE

MAXIMIZING YOUR SAVINGS ON THE PATH TO FINANCIAL FREEDOM THROUGH REAL ESTATE INVESTING

Copyright@2024

Andrews Otter

TABLE OF CONTENT

CHAPTER 1: UNDERSTANDING THE REAL ESTATE MARKET 11
   TYPES OF REAL ESTATE INVESTMENTS11
   RESIDENTIAL 11
CHAPTER 2: SETTING INVESTMENT GOALS44
   SHORT TERM VS. LONG TERM GOALS ..44
CHAPTER 3:. FINANCIAL PLANNING AND BUDGETING 66
   ASSESSING YOUR FINANCIAL SITUATION 66
CHAPTER 4: FINDING AND EVALUATING PROPERTIES 106
   PROPERTY SEARCH STRATEGIES 106
CHAPTER 5: MANAGING YOUR INVESTMENTS 127
   PROPERTY MANAGEMENT 127

INTRODUCTION TO REAL ESTATE INVESTING

1.1 What is Real Estate Investing?

- Definition: Investing in real estate includes shopping, owning, coping with, renting, or promoting homes for profit.
- Types of Real Estate: Includes residential, commercial, commercial, and land investments.

1.2 Why Invest in Real Estate?

- Tangible Asset: Unlike stocks or bonds, actual property is a bodily asset that you can see and touch.
- Potential for Appreciation: Real property homes can growth in price over time.
- Income Generation: Rental houses can offer a consistent circulation of profits.

- Tax Benefits: Real property traders can take gain of numerous tax deductions and advantages.

Leverage: Investors can use borrowed finances to increase their investment capacity.

1.3 Benefits of Real Estate Investing

- Diversification: Adding real estate on your funding portfolio can reduce chance and offer balance.
- Control: Unlike other investments, real estate offers a degree of manipulate over the belongings and its control.
- Inflation Hedge: Real estate frequently appreciates in value and generates condominium profits that may hold pace with inflation.
- Wealth Building: Long term actual estate investments can construct widespread wealth thru property appreciation and condo profits.

1.4 Common Misconceptions

- High Capital Requirement: Many agree with that actual estate making an investment requires widespread preliminary capital, but there are various ways to make investments with much less money down.
- It's a Passive Investment: While rental profits can be passive, dealing with properties frequently requires lively involvement or hiring a belongings supervisor.
- Guaranteed Profit: Real estate investing includes risks, inclusive of marketplace fluctuations and property control issues, and there are not any ensures of income.
- Immediate Returns: Real property investments regularly require patience, with returns realized through the years

through assets appreciation and rental earnings.

1.Five The Real Estate Market Landscape

- Market Segments: Understanding special kinds of real estate markets (residential, business, and so forth.) is important for making knowledgeable funding decisions.
- Economic Influences: Real estate markets are inspired by means of monetary elements consisting of hobby fees, employment rates, and nearby economic situations.
- Local vs. National Trends: Real estate markets can vary significantly from one region to any other, so it is important to analyze local market conditions.

1.6 Getting Started in Real Estate Investing

- Education: Learn approximately the real property marketplace, investment techniques, and monetary elements.

- Setting Goals: Define your investment goals, which include generating condo profits or achieving lengthy term appreciation.
- Building a Network: Connect with actual property agents, property managers, and different buyers to benefit insights and opportunities.

BENEFITS OF REAL ESTATE INVESTMENT

1. Tangible Asset

- Physical Presence: Real estate is a tangible asset that you may see and touch, that can provide a feel of safety and stability.
- Intrinsic Value: Unlike stocks or bonds, actual estate has intrinsic cost as a physical property.

2. Potential for Appreciation

- Value Increase: Real estate residences commonly appreciate through the years, doubtlessly main to vast profits while offered.

- Market Trends: Economic growth, infrastructure improvement, and community improvements can power belongings cost will increase.

3. Income Generation

- Rental Income: Properties can offer a regular move of income via lease payments, that may provide financial balance and cash flow.
- Diversified Income Streams: In addition to lease, profits can be generated from ancillary services like parking charges or laundry facilities.

4. Tax Benefits

- Deductions: Real estate buyers can advantage from diverse tax deductions, which include mortgage hobby, assets taxes, and depreciation.

- 1031 Exchange: Allows investors to defer capital gains taxes by reinvesting in like type houses.

5. Leverage
- Borrowed Funds: Investors can use borrowed budget to purchase houses, permitting them to manage a larger asset with a smaller quantity of their very own capital.
- Increased Returns: Leveraging can make bigger returns on investment, so long as the assets generates sufficient income to cowl the debt and charges.

6. Diversification
- Portfolio Balance: Real property provides diversification to an funding portfolio, which could reduce ordinary chance and volatility.
- Asset Class Variety: Offers an alternative to standard investments like

shares and bonds, supplying balance and stability.

7. Inflation Hedge
- Rising Value: Real property regularly appreciates in price and apartment earnings can boom with inflation, supporting buyers preserve purchasing electricity.
- Stable Cash Flow: Property rents may also upward thrust with inflation, presenting a steady income movement that adjusts with monetary conditions.

8. Wealth Building
- Long Term Growth: Over time, real property investments can build tremendous wealth through property appreciation and the accumulation of fairness.
- Generational Wealth: Real property may be surpassed down thru generations,

presenting long term monetary blessings for families.

9. Control Over Investment
- Active Management: Investors have direct control over assets management selections, which includes maintenance, tenant selection, and property improvements.
- Value Addition: Investors can boom property price thru renovations, improvements, and better management practices.

10. Community Impact
- Local Development: Real estate investments can make contributions to the improvement and improvement of communities, enhancing nearby infrastructure and services.

CHAPTER 1: UNDERSTANDING THE REAL ESTATE MARKET

TYPES OF REAL ESTATE INVESTMENTS

RESIDENTIAL

1. Overview of Residential Real Estate
- Definition: Residential real property entails residences used for living purposes, such as single own family homes, multi circle of relatives gadgets, condominiums, and apartments.
- Market Segments: Includes primary residences, apartment residences, excursion houses, and investment houses.

2. Types of Residential Properties
- Single Family Homes: Standby myself homes designed for one own family.

Common for both primary house and rental investments.
- Multi Family Units: Buildings with more than one separate housing units (e.G., duplexes, triplexes, and rental homes). Often used for apartment income.
- Condos: Individual gadgets inside a bigger building or complex, normally with shared not unusual areas and facilities. Can be proprietor occupied or rented out.
- Townhouses: Attached houses with shared walls but usually have character ownership of the assets. Can be a terrific condominium choice.

3. Benefits of Residential Real Estate Investment
- Steady Demand: People continually need locations to stay, main to a

consistent call for for apartment properties.

- Rental Income: Provides a reliable source of income thru month to month lease bills.
- Property Appreciation: Residential properties frequently recognize in fee over the years, growing capacity returns upon sale.
- Tax Advantages: Investors can gain from deductions on loan interest, property taxes, and depreciation.

4. Factors to Consider

- Location: The asset's region significantly influences its price and condo potential. Consider elements like proximity to services, faculties, and employment centers.
- Market Conditions: Analyze local real estate marketplace tendencies, together

with property values, condo prices, and vacancy rates.

- Property Management: Decide whether or not to control the belongings your self or lease a property management company. Effective control is crucial for retaining assets value and tenant delight.
- Financing: Explore financing options, inclusive of mortgages, to determine the quality method for funding your funding.

5. Strategies for Residential Real Estate Investment

- Buy and Hold: Purchase a belongings to hire out and keep it for lengthy time period appreciation and earnings era.
- Fix and Flip: Buy properties that want maintenance, enhance them, and promote them for a income. Requires information of upkeep and market timing.

- Rental Income: Focus on houses that offer a superb coins float via apartment income. Consider factors like belongings control and tenant screening.
- Vacation Rentals: Invest in houses in proper excursion locations and rent them out brief time period to tourists. This can generate higher condo income however may also require more control.

COMMERCIAL REAL ESTATE INVESTMENT

1. Overview of Commercial Real Estate

Definition: Commercial real estate includes homes used for commercial enterprise functions, such as workplace buildings, retail spaces, business facilities, and multi circle of relatives rental complexes with five or more devices.

TYPES OF COMMERCIAL PROPERTIES:
- Office Buildings: Spaces used for commercial enterprise operations,

ranging from small workplace suites to big skyscrapers.
- Retail Properties: Locations for agencies that promote goods without delay to purchasers, including purchasing facilities, strip department shops, and standalone shops.

Industrial Properties: Facilities used for manufacturing, warehousing, and distribution, inclusive of factories, warehouses, and distribution centers.
- Multi Family Residential: Apartment complexes with 5 or greater units, often taken into consideration business because of their length and income capacity.

2. Benefits of Commercial Real Estate Investment
- Higher Income Potential: Commercial homes often offer better condominium yields as compared to residential homes,

with lengthy term rentals and better rent costs.

- Long Term Leases: Commercial tenants usually sign longer rentals (310 years), offering extra solid and predictable profits streams.
- Triple Net Leases (NNN): In many business rentals, tenants pay for belongings taxes, coverage, and maintenance similarly to rent, decreasing the landlord's expenses.
- Diversification: Adding industrial houses on your funding portfolio can diversify income assets and decrease general danger.

3. Types of Commercial Real Estate Leases

- Gross Lease: The landlord covers all running fees, which include assets taxes, coverage, and preservation. The tenant pays a fixed rent.

- Net Lease: The tenant will pay lease plus a few or all of the working fees. Variants consist of unmarried net (N), double internet (NN), and triple net (NNN) leases.
- Percentage Lease: The tenant can pay a base rent plus a percentage of income revenue, commonly utilized in retail spaces.

4. Factors to Consider

- Location: Location is critical for commercial homes, affecting visibility, accessibility, and tenant demand. Proximity to foremost roads, transportation hubs, and enterprise districts is essential.
- Market Conditions: Analyze local industrial real property tendencies, inclusive of vacancy charges, condominium rates, and economic conditions. Understanding the business

environment allows in making informed selections.

- Tenant Demand: Assess the demand for commercial spaces within the region. Consider the kind of organizations which might be searching out area and the overall health of the local economy.
- Property Condition: Evaluate the situation of the property and any capacity for renovations or upgrades. Well maintained residences entice exquisite tenants and command higher rents.

5. Strategies for Commercial Real Estate Investment

- Buy and Hold: Purchase business properties to hire out and advantage from longtime period condominium profits and property appreciation.
- Value Add Investments: Buy properties that require upgrades or

repositioning, make improvements, and growth the belonging's value and condo income.

- Development Projects: Invest in new production or redevelopment projects to capitalize on rising markets or undeserved regions.
- Real Estate Investment Trusts (REITs): Invest in commercial actual property indirectly via REITs, which very own and manage commercial properties and distribute profits to shareholders.

6. Risks and Challenges

- Market Risk: Commercial real estate markets may be unstable and sensitive to financial downturns, affecting apartment earnings and property values.
- Tenant Risk: The fulfillment of commercial investments relies upon on tenant balance. Vacancies and tenant

defaults can impact coins glide and profitability.
- Property Management: Managing business homes may be complicated and can require specialized information, specifically with large or greater various belongings sorts.
- Financing Risk: Commercial homes often require large loans and better interest rates compared to residential homes, increasing financial chance.

MARKET ANALYSIS IN REAL ESTATE INVESTING

1. Introduction to Market Analysis
- Definition: Market analysis includes examining various factors that have an effect on actual property values and funding capability. It enables traders make knowledgeable choices via comparing present day market conditions, developments, and forecasts.

- Purpose: To perceive profitable investment possibilities, verify dangers, and understand marketplace dynamics that impact assets values and rental income.

2. Key Components of Market Analysis

- Economic Indicators: Analyze broader economic elements that affect the actual property market, inclusive of GDP increase, employment quotes, and inflation. Economic health influences assets demand and costs.
- Supply and Demand: Evaluate the balance among the supply of properties and the demand from buyers or renters. High call for with restrained deliver can pressure up charges and condo charges.
- Market Trends: Study historical and contemporary developments within the actual property market, inclusive of assets prices, rental quotes, and vacancy

charges. Recognize patterns which can indicate destiny marketplace behavior.

3. Local Market Analysis

- Neighborhood Analysis: Examine the precise community or sub market in which the assets is located. Consider elements like local services, faculties, crime charges, and transportation options.
- Comparable Sales (Comps): Analyze latest sales of comparable properties within the vicinity to decide market fee and price tendencies. Comps provide a benchmark for pricing and valuation.
- Rental Market: Assess neighborhood condo rates and demand for condominium homes. High apartment demand can lead to higher rental yields and decrease emptiness prices.

4. Property Specific Analysis
- Property Valuation: Determine the cost of a property the usage of techniques such as the sales contrast method, profits approach, or price technique. Accurate valuation allows in putting purchase fees and condominium costs.
- Income Potential: Calculate the capability income from the assets, which includes condo income and any extra sales sources. Consider the assets's capacity to generate fantastic coins glide.
- Operating Expenses: Estimate the ongoing fees associated with the assets, which include renovation, assets control, taxes, and coverage. Understanding charges is crucial for profitability.

5. Market Forecasting
- Future Trends: Analyze projected financial and actual property trends to

assume future market situations. Consider factors like population boom, infrastructure development, and modifications in neighborhood regulations.

- Investment Timing: Determine the most useful time to shop for or promote based on marketplace situations and forecasts. Timing can drastically effect investment returns.

6. Tools and Resources for Market Analysis

- Real Estate Databases: Use online structures and databases (e.G., Zillow, Realtor.Com, MLS) to access assets records, sales developments, and marketplace statistics.
- Economic Reports: Review reviews from government businesses, monetary think tanks, and actual property organizations for insights into broader economic and market situations.

- Local Real Estate Agents: Consult with neighborhood real property professionals who have in intensity know how of the marketplace and may provide treasured insights and facts.

7. Case Studies and Examples
- Successful Investments: Analyze case research of a success actual property investments to recognize market evaluation techniques and techniques used by different traders.
- Market Failures: Study examples of market downturns or failed investments to study from errors and avoid ability pitfalls.

ECONOMIC INDICATORS IN REAL ESTATE INVESTING

1. Introduction to Economic Indicators
- Definition: Economic signs are statistical metrics that replicate the overall fitness and direction of an

economy. They assist traders recognize marketplace situations and make informed choices concerning real estate investments.

- Importance: Economic indicators affect actual property markets by affecting belongings call for, values, and investment returns.

2. Key Economic Indicators

2.1 Gross Domestic Product (GDP)

- Definition: GDP measures the full monetary output of a rustic. It shows the general monetary fitness and boom rate.
- Impact on Real Estate: High GDP boom normally correlates with accelerated consumer spending, enterprise investments, and call for for real estate. Conversely, a declining GDP can signal monetary slowdowns and reduced actual property hobby.

2.2 Employment Rates

- Definition: Employment charges track the proportion of the running age populace that is hired. It includes metrics along with the unemployment price and job introduction figures.

- Impact on Real Estate: Higher employment fees generally lead to higher income degrees and expanded call for for housing. High unemployment can decrease housing demand and apartment income, impacting property values.

2.3 Inflation Rate

- Definition: Inflation measures the price at which the overall rate level of goods and services is rising. It is regularly tracked by means of indices inclusive of the Consumer Price Index (CPI).

- Impact on Real Estate: Moderate inflation can growth belongings values and rental profits. However, excessive inflation can erode purchasing energy and lead to higher hobby prices, which may negatively effect property affordability.

2.4 Interest Rates

- Definition: Interest costs are the cost of borrowing money, set by central banks and monetary institutions. Key fees encompass the federal finances price and loan prices.
- Impact on Real Estate: Lower hobby fees reduce the value of borrowing, making real estate investments greater lower priced and stimulating property demand. Conversely, higher interest fees can boom borrowing charges and slow down the real estate marketplace.

2. Five Housing Starts and Building Permits
- Definition: Housing starts off evolved talk over with the quantity of latest residential construction tasks initiated, at the same time as building lets in are approvals for brand spanking new production.
- Impact on Real Estate: High housing starts off evolved and building allows indicate a strong actual property market with developing demand. Low numbers can signal a slowdown in new production and capability shortages in housing deliver.

2.6 Consumer Confidence Index
- Definition: The Consumer Confidence Index measures the extent of confidence consumers have in the economy and their economic scenario.
- Impact on Real Estate: High consumer confidence can result in multiplied

spending and investment in actual estate. Low confidence may additionally result in reduced consumer spending and lower demand for houses.

LOCAL MARKET TRENDS IN REAL ESTATE INVESTING

1. Introduction to Local Market Trends

- Definition: Local marketplace developments talk to the precise situations and dynamics affecting real property markets inside a specific geographic place, together with a metropolis, community, or location.
- Importance: Understanding local marketplace tendencies is critical for making informed investment selections, as these tendencies can extensively effect assets values, rental income, and funding possibilities.

2. Key Local Market Trends

2.1 Property Values

- Trend Analysis: Examine historical and present day tendencies in belongings values inside the local market. Look at charge modifications through the years and examine them to broader market developments.

- Impact Factors: Factors influencing property values consist of neighborhood improvement, monetary situations, and deliver and call for dynamics.

2.2 Rental Rates

- Trend Analysis: Analyze tendencies in condo fees for unique assets kinds inside the local marketplace. This consists of monitoring average rents, changes through the years, and evaluating them to emptiness prices.

- Impact Factors: Rental prices can be encouraged by means of elements including local task growth, housing deliver, and tenant call for.

2.3 Vacancy Rates

- Trend Analysis: Assess the proportion of available apartment residences that are unoccupied. High emptiness quotes may additionally suggest oversupply or declining call for, at the same time as low vacancy rates recommend robust demand and probably better rents.
- Impact Factors: Factors affecting emptiness quotes consist of monetary conditions, belongings control practices, and nearby housing policies.

2.4 Development and Redevelopment Projects

- Trend Analysis: Identify ongoing and planned improvement or redevelopment tasks within the vicinity. New developments can growth property values and condominium call for, even

as redevelopment can revitalize neighborhoods.
- Impact Factors: Development projects are prompted by nearby authorities rules, infrastructure upgrades, and economic incentives.

2.5 Neighborhood Trends
- Trend Analysis: Examine traits unique to distinct neighborhoods, inclusive of gentrification, assets enhancements, or changes in neighborhood demographics.
- Impact Factors: Neighborhood developments can be pushed via elements like new services, changes in local services, and shifts in network alternatives.

2.6 Employment and Economic Growth
- Trend Analysis: Track neighborhood employment costs, enterprise increase, and economic improvement within the area. Strong financial growth and

process advent can result in increased call for for housing and higher assets values.
- Impact Factors: Economic increase is stimulated by using factors inclusive of most important employers, enterprise funding, and infrastructure upgrades.

2.7 Housing Supply and Demand
- Trend Analysis: Analyze the balance between housing supply and call for in the neighborhood marketplace. Consider factors together with new construction, housing inventory ranges, and populace boom.
- Impact Factors: Supply and call for dynamics can be affected by local zoning laws, housing affordability, and demographic traits.

2.8 Local Government Policies
- Trend Analysis: Review nearby government policies that effect real

property, including zoning guidelines, belongings taxes, rent manage, and housing incentives.

- Impact Factors: Changes in nearby regulations can affect assets values, investment opportunities, and normal marketplace conditions.

3. Tools and Resources for Analyzing Local Market Trends

- Real Estate Platforms: Use online actual property platforms to get entry to facts on belongings values, rental rates, and market trends.

- Local Real Estate Agents: Consult with nearby real property experts who have in depth expertise of the location and can provide insights into cutting edge market situations.

- Government Reports: Review reports and facts from neighborhood authorities agencies, financial development offices,

and planning departments for statistics on housing and financial trends.
- Market Research Reports: Analyze reviews from actual estate research corporations and industry corporations for certain market analyses and forecasts.

PROPERTY VALUATION IN REAL ESTATE INVESTING

1. Introduction to Property Valuation
- Definition: Property valuation is the system of determining the current marketplace value of a actual estate property. Accurate valuation is important for making knowledgeable funding selections, shopping for or selling homes, and assessing investment capability.
- Importance: Proper valuation helps investors set sensible purchase fees, estimate potential returns, and ensure

they are making sound investment decisions.

2. Common Valuation Methods

2.1 Sales Comparison Approach (Comparative Market Analysis)

- Definition: This approach estimates a property's value based totally on the sale costs of comparable properties (comps) within the same location.

Process:

- Identify Comps: Select recently sold residences with similar traits (area, size, type, situation) to the problem property.
- Adjust for Differences: Make adjustments for variations among the comps and the challenge belongings, together with varying square pictures, services, or circumstance.
- Determine Value: Calculate an average or median adjusted value to

estimate the marketplace value of the concern assets.

- Best Used For: Residential residences and properties in set up markets wherein comparable income are comfortably available.

2.2 Income Approach

- Definition: This technique estimates a asset's cost based on its potential to generate earnings, usually used for investment homes consisting of condominium apartments or commercial properties.

Process:

- Calculate Net Operating Income (NOI): Determine the asset's annual earnings (rents) minus running charges (upkeep, control expenses, taxes, insurance).
- Apply Capitalization Rate (Cap Rate): Use a capitalization fee, which

displays the return on investment for comparable homes, to convert the NOI into a assets value. The system is:

$$\text{Value} = \frac{\text{NOI}}{\text{Cap Rate}}$$

Determine Cap Rate: The cap price is derived from marketplace records and displays investor expectations for similar properties.

Best Used For: Income generating properties, including condo houses, industrial real estate, and multi own family devices.

2.3 Cost Approach

- Definition: This technique estimates a property's fee based totally at the price to replace or reproduce the assets, minus depreciation.

Process:
- Calculate Replacement Cost: Estimate the cost to construct a comparable property with the equal materials and exceptional.
- Subtract Depreciation: Deduct depreciation for bodily put on and tear, purposeful obsolescence, and external elements (e.G., neighborhood decline).
- Add Land Value: Include the cost of the land on which the property is situated.
- Best Used For: Unique or newly built houses in which similar income are constrained, and in conditions wherein the value of creation is a big component.

3. Factors Affecting Property Valuation
- Location: Proximity to amenities, transportation, and overall community desirability can drastically impact belongings value.

- Property Size and Condition: Larger homes and those in higher circumstance usually have higher values. Consider factors just like the variety of bedrooms, lavatories, and usual protection.
- Market Conditions: Current market tendencies, together with supply and call for dynamics, interest prices, and monetary situations, can affect property values.
- Economic Indicators: Broader monetary elements, together with GDP boom, employment fees, and inflation, affect real estate values.

CHAPTER 2: SETTING INVESTMENT GOALS

SHORT TERM VS. LONG TERM GOALS

RISK TOLERANCE IN REAL ESTATE INVESTING

1. Introduction to Risk Tolerance
- Definition: Risk tolerance refers to an investor's potential and willingness to endure potential losses or volatility of their investments. In real property, this involves balancing ability returns with the risks associated with exceptional kinds of residences and funding techniques.
- Importance: Understanding your hazard tolerance helps manual investment choices, making sure that

your actual property portfolio aligns together with your financial goals,

2. Factors Influencing Risk Tolerance

2.1 Financial Situation

- Income and Savings: Investors with higher incomes and big financial savings can typically come up with the money for to take on more risk, as they have got a monetary cushion to soak up capability losses.
- Debt Levels: High ranges of debt may additionally reduce an investor's ability to take on danger, as servicing debt calls for solid income and limits to be had capital for investments.

2.2 Investment Goals

- Short Term vs. Long Term Goals: Investors with lengthy time period goals (e.G., retirement making plans) may be more tolerant of quicklime period volatility, whilst those with quick term desires (e.G., saving for a down charge) may additionally decide on lower danger investments.

- Return Expectations: High go back expectancy often come with higher chance. Investors searching for big capital appreciation can also need to just accept greater chance, even as those targeted on regular profits might also opt for decrease danger homes.

2.3 Experience and Knowledge

- Real Estate Knowledge: Experienced buyers who apprehend marketplace dynamics, belongings management, and investment techniques may additionally sense greater cushy taking up chance.

- Past Experiences: Previous success or failure in real property making an investment can have an effect on an investor's consolation level with chance. Those who've experienced losses can be greater cautious, whilst people with a success investments can be more inclined to take risks.

2.Four Age and Time Horizon

- Younger Investors: Investors with a longer time horizon have more time to get over potential losses, letting them take on higher hazard investments.
- Older Investors: As buyers technique retirement or other economic milestones, they'll opt for decrease danger investments to preserve capital and ensure stable profits.

2.5 Psychological Comfort

- Risk Aversion: Some investors are clearly greater threat averse and may prefer more secure investments, although it means accepting decrease returns.
- Stress and Anxiety: High danger investments can result in pressure and

anxiety, especially in the course of market downturns. Understanding your emotional response to chance is crucial in deciding on appropriate investments.

3. Assessing Your Risk Tolerance

3.1 Self Assessment Tools

- Questionnaires: Use online risk tolerance questionnaires that compare your comfort with funding volatility, capacity losses, and financial goals.
- Scenario Analysis: Consider how you will react in diverse marketplace scenarios, consisting of a big property value decline or surprising vacancy in a rental belongings.

3.2 Professional Guidance

- Financial Advisors: Consult with a economic advisor or real estate investment expert who can assist examine your threat tolerance and propose suitable funding strategies.

Real Estate Mentors: Experienced investors or mentors can offer insights into handling threat and making knowledgeable choices based

INVESTMENT STRATEGIES IN REAL ESTATE INVESTING

1. Introduction to Investment Strategies

- Definition: Investment strategies in real estate are plans or techniques designed to achieve specific economic desires through property investments.
- Importance: Selecting the proper investment approach is critical for maximizing returns whilst coping with risks. It helps investors awareness their efforts and sources on accomplishing their monetary goals.

2. Common Real Estate Investment Strategies

2.1 Buy and Hold

- Definition: The purchase and preserve approach entails shopping homes with the goal of conserving them lengthy time period, incomes apartment earnings, and profiting from assets appreciation over the years.

Key Features:

- Rental Income: Generate regular coins float through leasing the property to tenants.
- Appreciation: Potential for substantial lengthy time period profits as assets values increase through the years.
- Tax Benefits: Investors may additionally advantage from tax deductions on loan interest, belongings taxes, and depreciation.

- Best For: Investors with a protracted time period outlook who are searching for passive earnings and sluggish wealth accumulation.

2.2 Fix and Flip

- Definition: The restoration and turn strategy entails shopping for distressed or undervalued residences, renovating them, and then selling them at a better charge for a profit.

Key Features:

- Short Term Profits: Potential for excessive returns inside a brief time body, typically some months to a year.
- Renovation Skills: Requires understanding of production, design, and market tendencies to successfully enhance assets value.
- Market Timing: Success depends on the capability to shop for low and sell

excessive, regularly in swiftly appreciating markets.

Best For: Investors with experience in real property, creation, or home development who are snug with higher threat and active control.

2.3 Rental Property Investment

Definition: This strategy specializes in obtaining residential or commercial residences to lease out to tenants, generating ongoing apartment earnings.

Key Features:
- Cash Flow: Steady income circulation from month to month lease payments.
- Property Management: May require active involvement in handling tenants, upkeep, and belongings protection, or using a property control organization.
- Leverage: Ability to apply financing (mortgages) to acquire houses,

potentially growing returns on investment.

Best For: Investors in search of consistent coins go with the flow and the ability for belongings appreciation, who are willing to control or oversee belongings operations.

2.4 Real Estate Investment Trusts (REITs)

Definition: REITs are corporations that very own, perform, or finance profits producing actual estate. Investors should buy stocks in a REIT, gaining exposure to real property without immediately proudly owning belongings.

Key Features:

- Liquidity: REIT stocks are typically traded on stock exchanges, offering greater liquidity compared to direct property possession.
- Diversification: Invest in a portfolio of properties, lowering hazard as

compared to making an investment in a unmarried belongings.

- Dividends: REITs are required to distribute maximum of their earnings to shareholders, supplying everyday dividend payments.

Best For: Investors seeking out publicity to actual estate with out the obligations of assets possession, or those looking for a extra liquid funding.

2.5 Real Estate Crowdfunding

- Definition: Real property crowdfunding lets in a couple of investors to pool their money to spend money on larger real property tasks. This is frequently facilitated through online structures.

Key Features:

- Lower Capital Requirements: Investors can participate with smaller amounts of capital as compared to direct assets possession.

- Access to Larger Deals: Enables participation in huge industrial or residential projects that would be inaccessible to individual buyers.

Passive Investment: Typically requires little to no active control from person traders.

Best For: Investors looking for a passive, lower fee way to invest in real property, or those inquisitive about particular sorts of actual estate projects.

BUY AND HOLD STRATEGY IN REAL ESTATE INVESTING

1. Introduction to Buy and Hold Strategy

- Definition: The purchase and hold method involves buying real estate properties with the goal of preserving onto them for an extended duration, generating condominium earnings, and making the most of belongings appreciation over the years.

- Objective: The number one aim is to create lengthy time period wealth via regular cash drift from leases and the sluggish boom in assets price.

2. Key Features of Buy and Hold Strategy

2.1 Rental Income

- Steady Cash Flow: The belongings is rented out to tenants, offering a everyday profits stream. This may be used to cover mortgage payments, property upkeep, and other charges, with the ability for earnings.
- Passive Income: Over time, as the mortgage is paid down and rents potentially growth, the assets can grow to be a full size source of passive earnings.

2.2 Property Appreciation
- Long Term Value Increase: Real property normally appreciates in fee over the years, mainly in markets with strong call for. Holding onto the property lets in investors to gain from this appreciation after they finally sell.
- Equity Growth: As the belongings fee increases and the loan stability decreases, the owner builds fairness, which may be leveraged for future investments.

2.3 Tax Benefits
- Depreciation: Investors can deduct the cost of the belongings over its beneficial life, decreasing taxable income. This is a giant tax advantage specific to actual property.
- Mortgage Interest Deduction: Interest paid at the mortgage is commonly tax deductible, further decreasing the investor's tax burden.

- Other Deductions: Property taxes, protection fees, and control prices also are deductible, enhancing the overall go back on funding.

2.4 Leverage
- Financing the Purchase: The buy and keep approach regularly involves the use of mortgage financing, allowing buyers to govern a precious asset with exceptionally little capital prematurely.
- Amplifying Returns: By the use of leverage, traders can potentially increase their return on fairness, as they earn apartment profits and appreciation on the complete value of the belongings, no longer simply the element they've paid for in coins.

3. Types of Properties Suitable for Buy and Hold

3.1 Residential Properties

Single Family Homes: Popular for first time real property investors, supplying regular call for and less complicated control.

Multi Family Properties: Include duplexes, triplexes, and condominium homes, providing more than one earnings streams and often better returns.

3.2 Commercial Properties

- Office Buildings: Can offer higher condominium profits, though commonly require extra control and longer lease phrases.
- Retail Spaces: Suitable for places with strong customer site visitors, though difficulty to monetary fluctuations.

3.3 Mixed Use Properties

Combination of Residential and Commercial: These residences offer diversified income streams and can be extra resilient to marketplace adjustments.

4. Risks and Challenges of Buy and Hold Strategy

RENTAL PROPERTIES IN REAL ESTATE INVESTING

1. Introduction to Rental Properties

- Definition: Rental homes are real property investments in which the owner rentals out residential or business area to tenants in trade for rental profits. This method specializes in generating consistent coins flow at the same time as doubtlessly profiting from belongings appreciation through the years.
- Objective: The primary goal is to construct a portfolio of earnings producing homes that offer consistent returns and longtime period financial increase.

2. Types of Rental Properties

2.1 Residential Rental Properties

　Single Family Homes: These are standalone residences rented out to individual households or tenants. They are often easier to manipulate and attract lengthy time period tenants.

- Multi Family Properties: These include duplexes, triplexes, and condominium buildings, where more than one units are rented out to exclusive tenants. They provide the capacity for higher condominium earnings and spread risk throughout more than one devices.
- Condominiums and Townhouses: These homes are individually owned units inside a bigger complicated, with shared amenities and preservation prices. They can entice tenants seeking out a network dwelling surroundings.

2.2 Commercial Rental Properties

- Office Buildings: Spaces rented out to corporations for office use. These residences commonly have longer hire phrases and can offer solid profits.

- Retail Spaces: Properties rented to agencies for retail functions, consisting of shops or eating places. Location is crucial for those investments, because it at once influences foot traffic and tenant success.

- Industrial Properties: Warehouses, factories, and different commercial spaces rented to companies. These homes often require specialized know how however can yield excessive returns.

2.3 Short Term Rental Properties

- Vacation Rentals: Properties rented out on a short term foundation, frequently to travelers or travelers. Platforms like Airbnb have made short time period leases a famous and doubtlessly lucrative alternative.

- Corporate Housing: Furnished residences rented out for brief time period remains, often to business tourists or brief people.

3. Key Considerations for Rental Property Investment

3.1 Location

- Neighborhood Quality: Properties in suited neighborhoods with desirable colleges, low crime charges, and get right of entry to to services tend to attract higher nice tenants and yield better returns.
- Proximity to Employment Centers: Properties close to commercial enterprise districts or regions with sturdy process increase frequently see higher call for from renters.

- Market Trends: Understanding neighborhood market trends, such as populace growth, development plans, and economic situations, can help pick out worthwhile apartment markets.

3.2 Financing Options

- Mortgages: Most apartment homes are financed with mortgages, where the apartment income is used to cowl loan payments. Choosing the right loan kind (constant vs. Adjustable charge) is vital.
- Down Payment Requirements: Rental residences regularly require better down bills than number one residences, commonly round 2030%.
- Loan Terms: Investors need to remember the loan terms, interest costs, and amortization duration when financing a apartment belongings.

3.3 Property Management

- Self Management vs. Professional Management: Investors need to decide whether or not to manipulate the property themselves or hire a property control employer. Self management can shop cash however requires time and effort, while professional management offers comfort and knowledge at a cost.
- Tenant Screening: Effective tenant screening is crucial to avoid troubles consisting of past due payments or belongings harm. This consists of checking credit score history, employment status, and condominium references.

CHAPTER 3:. FINANCIAL PLANNING AND BUDGETING

ASSESSING YOUR FINANCIAL SITUATION

FINANCING OPTIONS IN REAL ESTATE INVESTING

1. Introduction to Financing Options
- Definition: Financing options in real property consult with the various strategies investors can use to fund the acquisition of homes. These alternatives range from conventional financial institution loans to creative financing techniques, every with its personal set of terms, necessities, and blessings.
- Importance: Understanding the available financing options is vital for maximizing investment returns, dealing with cash float, and minimizing danger.

2. Traditional Financing Options

2.1 Conventional Mortgage Loans

- Definition: A traditional loan is a loan that is not insured or assured through the federal authorities. It is generally presented through banks, credit unions, and loan creditors.

Key Features:

- Down Payment: Typically calls for a 20% down fee to keep away from private mortgage insurance (PMI), although a few creditors provide loans with lower down payments.
- Interest Rates: Fixed or adjustable interest quotes, with constant fee loans offering stability in payments over the years.
- Loan Terms: Commonly supplied in 15, 20, or 3012 months terms, with longer phrases resulting in lower month

to month payments however higher basic interest expenses.

Best For: Investors with robust credit score scores, stable profits, and the ability to make a massive down payment.

2.2 FHA Loans

- Definition: The Federal Housing Administration (FHA) offers loans that are insured by way of the government, making them accessible to debtors with lower credit score scores and smaller down payments.

Key Features:

- Lower Down Payments: Typically as little as 3.5%, making it simpler for first time traders to buy assets.
- Mortgage Insurance Premiums (MIP): Requires each an upfront top rate and an annual top class, which will increase the general fee of the loan.

- Loan Limits: FHA loans have limits on the amount that may be borrowed, which vary with the aid of place.
- Best For: First time investors or people with limited budget for a down payment.

2.3 VA Loans

- Definition: VA loans are mortgage loans guaranteed by way of the U.S. Department of Veterans Affairs, available to eligible veterans, lively obligation provider contributors, and some contributors of the National Guard and Reserves.

Key Features:
- No Down Payment: Allows eligible borrowers to buy residences without a down charge.
- No Private Mortgage Insurance (PMI): VA loans do no longer require PMI, lowering monthly bills.

- Competitive Interest Rates: Typically offer decrease hobby quotes as compared to conventional loans.

Best For: Veterans and lively obligation navy personnel seeking to invest in actual property.

3. Alternative Financing Options

3.1 Hard Money Loans

Definition: Hard cash loans are brief time period loans supplied by means of personal lenders, secured by using the property itself in place of the borrower's creditworthiness.

Key Features:
- Quick Approval: Faster approval and investment compared to standard loans, regularly inside days.
- Higher Interest Rates: Typically have better interest rates and shorter phrases (624 months) than conventional loans.
- Used for: Commonly used for restore and flip tasks, wherein investors want

brief get entry to to funds for assets buy and preservation.

Best For: Investors who need short financing and are snug with higher interest costs and short reimbursement intervals.

CONVENTIONAL LOANS IN REAL ESTATE INVESTING

1. Introduction to Conventional Loans

- Definition: A conventional loan is a mortgage that isn't insured or assured by using any government agency, such as the Federal Housing Administration (FHA) or Veterans Affairs (VA). These loans are usually supplied with the aid of personal lenders, including banks, credit score unions, and loan agencies.
- Importance: Conventional loans are one of the maximum common financing options for real estate traders due to their flexibility, competitive interest rates, and potential for lower universal fees.

2. Key Features of Conventional Loans

2.1 Down Payment Requirements

- Standard Down Payment: Typically, traditional loans require a down price of as a minimum 20% of the assets's purchase rate to keep away from personal loan insurance (PMI). However, a few creditors provide conventional loans with down bills as low as three% to 5%, in particular for first time home buyers.
- Avoiding PMI: A down price of 20% or extra allows investors to keep away from PMI, that can upload full size prices to month to month bills.

2.2 Interest Rates

- Fixed Rate Loans: The hobby charge remains the equal at some stage in the lifestyles of the mortgage, supplying balance in month to month bills. Fixed fee terms are normally available in 15, 20, or 30 years.

- Adjustable Rate Mortgages (ARMs): The hobby rate is constant for an preliminary duration (usually 5, 7, or 10 years) after which adjusts yearly primarily based on market conditions. ARMs usually provide decrease preliminary charges however can bring about better payments if hobby prices upward thrust.

2.3 Loan Terms

- Short Term Loans: Common terms encompass 15 or two decades, which bring about higher month to month bills but decrease basic hobby charges.
- Long Term Loans: The maximum commonplace term is 30 years, which affords lower monthly bills, making it less complicated to manage coins flow,

but will increase the entire hobby paid over the lifestyles of the mortgage.

2.4 Credit Score Requirements

Minimum Credit Score: Conventional loans usually require a minimal credit score score of round 620. However, debtors with higher credit score ratings (above 740) are possibly to obtain extra favorable interest rates and phrases.

Impact on Interest Rates: A higher credit score score can drastically lower the interest price, lowering the general cost of the loan.

2.5 Debt to Income Ratio (DTI)

- Standard DTI Ratios: Lenders commonly choose a DTI ratio (the proportion of your gross monthly income that is going toward debt bills) of 36% or much less. However, some lenders might also permit ratios as much as 43% or higher, relying on different

elements like credit score rating and down payment.
- Importance: A lower DTI ratio can improve your chances of mortgage approval and bring about better loan phrases.

3. Advantages of Conventional Loans

3.1 Flexibility
- Property Types: Conventional loans may be used to finance a wide variety of properties, which includes unmarried circle of relatives houses, multifamily units, condos, and excursion properties.
- Investment Properties: Conventional loans are broadly to be had for funding homes, making them a famous desire for real estate traders.

3.2 Potential for Lower Costs
- No Upfront Fees: Unlike authorities sponsored loans, conventional loans do no longer require in advance mortgage

insurance charges (like FHA loans) or funding prices (like VA loans).
- No Mortgage Insurance with 20% Down: Avoiding PMI with a 20% down payment can substantially reduce the price of the loan through the years.

3.3 Competitive Interest Rates
- Market Driven Rates: Conventional loans regularly offer aggressive interest charges which are decided by means of market conditions and the borrower's creditworthiness.

4. Challenges of Conventional Loans

4.1 Stricter Qualification Requirements
- Higher Credit Standards: Borrowers commonly need a robust credit history and higher credit score scores to qualify for conventional loans, specially for the pleasant charges.
- Larger Down Payments: The requirement for a larger down fee (often

20%) may be a barrier for some buyers, particularly first time buyers.

4.2 PMI for Low Down Payments

Private Mortgage Insurance (PMI): If the down fee is less than 20%, borrowers must pay for PMI, which provides to the monthly mortgage price. This coverage protects the lender in case of borrower default however does no longer advantage the borrower at once.

5. When to Choose a Conventional Loan

- Strong Credit and Financial Stability: Ideal for investors with desirable credit score rankings, low DTI ratios, and the ability to make a sizeable down price.
- Long Term Investment Strategy: Suitable for those planning to preserve the assets longtime period, cashing in on fixed charge stability and sluggish fairness growth.

PRIVATE LENDERS IN REAL ESTATE INVESTING

1. Introduction to Private Lenders

- Definition: Private lenders are people or corporations that offer loans immediately to real property traders, bypassing traditional monetary establishments like banks or credit score unions. These loans are generally quick term and secured by way of the property itself.

- Importance: Private lending gives flexibility, velocity, and accessibility, making it a precious alternative for investors, specifically folks who need brief financing or have difficulty securing conventional loans.

2. Key Features of Private Lending

2.1 Speed of Funding

- Quick Approval: Private lenders can often approve and fund loans a lot faster than traditional banks, once in a while inside a be counted of days. This is in particular advantageous in aggressive markets where short motion is important.

- Streamlined Process: Private loans generally contain less office work and less bureaucratic hurdles, making the system more trustworthy and green.

2.2 Flexible Terms

- Negotiable Terms: Unlike traditional loans, wherein terms are often standardized, nonpublic loans offer extra flexibility. Loan terms, interest fees, and reimbursement schedules may be negotiated among the borrower and the lender to fit specific wishes.

- Short Term Nature: Private loans are normally short time period, frequently ranging from six months to 3 years. This is ideal for traders looking to flip homes or the ones needing bridge financing.

2.3 Higher Interest Rates

- Increased Cost: Due to the higher chance worried, personal loans regularly include better hobby fees compared to traditional mortgages. Rates can vary significantly depending on the lender and the specifics of the deal, but they commonly variety from 8% to 15% or greater.

Cost vs. Convenience: The higher fee is often justified via the velocity and flexibility presented with the aid of private creditors, particularly in time sensitive or high capacity investments.

2.4 Collateral Based Lending

- Property as Security: Private creditors commonly focus at the value of the assets getting used as collateral instead of the borrower's creditworthiness. This makes private loans accessible to investors with much less than ideal credit or unconventional earnings assets.

- Loan to Value Ratio (LTV): Private lenders often require a lower LTV ratio (usually sixty five% to 75%), which means borrowers might also need a massive down charge or equity inside the belongings.

2.5 Risk Management

- Higher Risk for Lenders: Since personal loans are often granted to borrowers who might not qualify for traditional financing, creditors tackle extra hazard. To mitigate this, they'll impose stricter terms or require additional collateral.

- Default Consequences: If the borrower defaults, the lender can foreclose on the property, as the loan is secured by the real estate itself. This makes it critical for debtors to carefully investigate their capacity to repay the loan in the agreed phrases.

3. Types of Private Lenders

3.1 Individual Private Lenders

Friends and Family: Loans from pals, family members, or associates may be arranged informally or with the help of a legal settlement to formalize phrases.

- Private Investors: Wealthy individuals or professional investors who lend their personal cash to actual property traders, often looking for better returns than traditional investments.

3.2 Private Lending Companies

- Specialized Firms: These companies attention on providing loans to real property investors, often with a focal point on fix and flip tasks, apartment property acquisitions, or industrial tendencies.

- Pool of Investors: Some nonpublic lending companies perform by way of pooling price range from a couple of traders, spreading the danger throughout numerous projects.

3. Three Hard Money Lenders

- Definition: Hard money lenders are a selected form of private lender who gives short term loans secured by way of actual estate. These loans are usually used for quick transactions, along with property flips or when traditional financing isn't always an choice.
- Characteristics: Hard cash loans are recognized for their excessive interest fees, quick intervals, and reliance on the asset's price in preference to the borrower's credit records.

4. When to Use Private Lenders

4.1 Fix and Flip Projects

- Short Term Financing Needs: Private loans are best for traders who plan to speedy renovate and promote a property, because the mortgage terms align with the fast timeline of such initiatives.
- Flexibility: The capacity to barter phrases lets in traders to structure the loan to fit the unique needs of the project.

CROWDFUNDING IN REAL ESTATE INVESTING

1. Introduction to Crowdfunding

- Definition: Real estate crowdfunding is a technique of elevating capital for actual estate investments through pooling small quantities of money from a huge quantity of traders, generally through a web platform. This technique lets in character traders to participate in actual estate offers that would otherwise be inaccessible due to high capital necessities.

- Importance: Crowdfunding democratizes actual estate making an investment by means of enabling participation from a huge range of traders, such as those with confined price range, even as offering get admission to to diverse actual estate possibilities.

2. How Real Estate Crowdfunding Works

2.1 Online Platforms

- Intermediaries: Crowdfunding structures act as intermediaries among real property developers or sponsors and person investors. They vet funding possibilities and deal with the logistics of raising and managing budget.
- Examples: Popular actual estate crowdfunding structures encompass

Fund rise, Realty Mogul, Crowd Street, and Peer Street.

2.2 Investment Structure

- Equity Investments: Investors buy stocks in a selected assets or a portfolio of properties, turning into partial owners. Returns come from condo earnings, assets appreciation, or profits from a sale.
- Debt Investments: Investors lend money to a actual estate project in alternate for constant hobby payments, much like holding a mortgage. These are generally considered lower risk however offer lower returns in comparison to equity investments.

2.3 Minimum Investment Requirements

- Low Entry Points: Unlike traditional real property making an investment, crowdfunding systems regularly have low minimum investment requirements,

ranging from $500 to $five,000, making it reachable to greater people.
- Scalability: Investors can start with a small amount and gradually growth their funding as they grow to be more snug with the platform and the dangers worried.

3. Types of Real Estate Crowdfunding

3.1 Residential Properties

- Single Family Homes: Investments in unmarried own family condo houses, frequently pooled into portfolios, where buyers percentage in the condominium income and belongings appreciation.
- Multi Family Units: Crowdfunding systems may also provide opportunities to spend money on condominium complexes or other multifamily residential homes.

3.2 Commercial Properties

- Office Buildings: Investments in business workplace spaces, that can provide higher returns however additionally bring higher chance due to market fluctuations and tenant turnover.

BUDGETING FOR REAL ESTATE INVESTMENTS

1. Introduction to Budgeting for Real Estate Investments

- Definition: Budgeting for real property investments involves planning and allocating economic resources to make certain that every one fees associated with shopping, coping with, and keeping a belongings are protected. This technique is essential for maximizing returns and minimizing monetary chance.
- Importance: A properly based budget helps buyers recognize the overall fee of

ownership, keep away from sudden expenses, and make knowledgeable decisions about their investments.

2. Key Components of a Real Estate Investment Budget

2.1 Acquisition Costs

- Property Purchase Price: The maximum huge issue of the finances, which includes the agreed upon rate for the property.
- Down Payment: Typically 20% or extra of the acquisition fee for traditional loans, although this could vary depending on the financing approach.
- Closing Costs: These consist of numerous expenses related to finalizing the property purchase, consisting of loan origination prices, appraisal prices, identify insurance, and criminal fees. Closing expenses commonly range from

2% to five% of the property's purchase rate.

- Inspection and Appraisal Fees: Fees for a professional inspection and appraisal to evaluate the belonging's condition and marketplace value.

2.2 Financing Costs

- Loan Origination Fees: A price charged by means of the lender for processing the mortgage application, typically zero.Five% to one% of the loan quantity.
- Interest Payments: Regular payments at the borrowed quantity, in order to rely upon the mortgage's interest price and time period.
- Private Mortgage Insurance (PMI): If the down payment is much less than 20%, PMI can be required, including to the monthly value of the mortgage.

- Points: Some investors may pick out to pay cut price factors in advance to lessen the loan's interest rate over its time period. Each factor normally costs 1% of the loan quantity.

2.3 Rehabilitation and Improvement Costs

- Renovation and Repair Costs: If the property needs maintenance or updates, budgeting for those fees is vital. This ought to encompass structural repairs, beauty updates, or main renovations.
- Permits and Licenses: Any important preservation may additionally require allows or licenses, that can add to the overall price.

Contingency Fund: A reserve for surprising fees at some stage in preservation, generally round 10% to 20% of the total renovation finances.

2.4 Operating Costs

- Property Management Fees: If using a assets control organization, charges commonly range from eight% to 12% of the month to month rental earnings.
- Maintenance and Repairs: Ongoing prices to hold the property, consisting of landscaping, ordinary upkeep, and emergency fixes. A common rule of thumb is to budget 1% to two% of the property fee yearly for renovation.
- Utilities: Costs for utilities that are the duty of the property proprietor, which include water, power, gas, and trash removal.
- Insurance: Property insurance to shield in opposition to damage, legal responsibility, and different dangers. The value will vary primarily based on the belonging's location, cost, and insurance kind.

Property Taxes: Annual taxes levied by using nearby governments based on the belonging's assessed price.

2.5 Vacancy and Reserve Funds

Vacancy Rate: A budgeted amount to cover intervals when the belongings isn't always producing condominium earnings. Typically, traders finances for a emptiness charge of five% to 10% of capacity rental profits.

DOWN PAYMENTS IN REAL ESTATE INVESTING

1. Introduction to Down Payments

- Definition: A down fee is the initial payment made by means of a client while shopping a property, representing a portion of the whole buy fee. The the rest of the price is generally financed thru a loan or loan.

Importance: The length of the down price impacts diverse components of the funding, along with the mortgage phrases, month to month loan bills, interest charges, and the necessity of additional costs like mortgage insurance.

2. Typical Down Payment Requirements

2.1 Conventional Loans

- Standard Down Payment: For conventional loans, the standard down payment is commonly 20% of the asset's purchase charge. This amount facilitates borrowers avoid paying nonpublic loan insurance (PMI).
- Lower Down Payment Options: Some lenders offer conventional loans with down payments as low as three% to 5%, mainly for first time home buyers. However, these loans usually require PMI till the borrower reaches 20% fairness inside the property.

2.2 FHA Loans

- Low Down Payment: FHA loans are designed to assist buyers with lower credit score ratings or confined budget, offering down payments as little as three.Five% of the purchase fee.
- Mortgage Insurance Premiums (MIP): Borrowers should pay each an in advance premium and annual mortgage insurance rates, regardless of the down charge length, making it greater high priced over time compared to traditional loans with higher down bills.

2.3 VA Loans

- No Down Payment: VA loans, to be had to eligible veterans and lively duty military personnel, usually require no down charge. This is a substantial gain, allowing buyers to finance a hundred% of the property's buy price.

- No PMI: Unlike other low or no down price options, VA loans do not require nonpublic loan coverage.

2.4 USDA Loans

- Zero Down Payment: USDA loans, designed for rural and suburban home buyers, also permit for 0 down payment, making home ownership more reachable in specified regions.
- Income Limits: These loans have particular income limits and are supposed for low to moderate income consumers.

3. Factors Influencing Down Payment Amounts

3.1 Loan Type

- Conventional vs. Government Backed Loans: Conventional loans frequently require larger down payments as compared to government backed loans like FHA, VA, and USDA loans, which have greater lenient necessities.

3.2 Credit Score

- Impact on Down Payment: A better credit score score can lead to greater favorable loan phrases, doubtlessly decreasing the required down fee. Conversely, a decrease credit score score would possibly necessitate a bigger down price to offset the lender's risk.

3.3 Investment Property vs. Primary Residence

- Higher Requirements for Investment Properties: Down price necessities for investment residences are commonly higher, usually around 20% to 25%, in comparison to primary residences, which could regularly be purchased with as little as three% to five% down.

3.4 Lender Policies

Variation Among Lenders: Different lenders can also have various rules on down bills, specifically for unconventional properties, like multi circle of relatives units or fixer uppers.

4. Advantages of Larger Down Payments

4.1 Lower Monthly Payments

- Reduced Principal: A large down charge reduces the mortgage quantity, leading to decrease monthly mortgage bills.
- Interest Savings: With a smaller mortgage balance, debtors pay much less interest over the existence of the mortgage, doubtlessly saving lots of dollars.

4.2 Better Loan Terms

- Lower Interest Rates: Borrowers who make larger down bills regularly qualify for lower interest quotes, as they pose much less chance to the lender.

CLOSING COSTS IN REAL ESTATE TRANSACTIONS

1. Introduction to Closing Costs

- Definition: Closing expenses are charges and costs that buyers and sellers incur to finalize a real estate transaction. These prices are paid at the remaining meeting, in which the possession of the assets is officially transferred from the seller to the consumer.

- Importance: Understanding and budgeting for closing charges is important for each buyers and dealers to make sure a easy transaction and avoid sudden charges.

2. Common Closing Costs for Buyers

2.1 Loan Related Costs

- Loan Origination Fee: A charge charged through the lender for processing the loan utility, typically round zero.5% to at least one% of the loan quantity.

- Appraisal Fee: A rate for an unbiased appraisal of the property's cost, which allows the lender determine the loan quantity. Typically tiers from $three hundred to $six hundred.
- Credit Report Fee: A fee for obtaining the borrower's credit record to assess creditworthiness, generally between $30 and $50.

2.2 Inspection Costs

- Home Inspection Fee: A rate for a radical inspection of the belonging's condition, which includes structural, mechanical, and safety components. Usually stages from $three hundred to $500.
- Pest Inspection Fee: If required, this fee covers the inspection for pests like

termites. Typically stages from $50 to $one hundred fifty.

2.3 Title and Legal Fees

- Title Search and Title Insurance: A rate for looking the assets's title records to make certain there are not any splendid claims or liens, and a price for name insurance to protect towards destiny claims. Title coverage costs vary but are often among $three hundred and $1,000.
- Attorney Fees: Fees for legal offerings associated with the transaction, if relevant. These costs can range extensively depending on the complexity of the transaction and the attorney's price.

2.4 Escrow Fees

- Escrow Fee: A fee for the offerings of an escrow agency that manages the price range and files during the transaction. This rate is usually break up between the consumer and seller and generally tiers from $three hundred to $1,000.

2.5 Prepaid Costs

- Property Taxes: Prepayment of a part of property taxes for the cutting edge yr, based on the ultimate date. The amount varies depending on nearby tax prices and the time of year.
- Homeowners Insurance: Prepayment of house owners coverage for the primary yr. Costs vary primarily based on the property's area, length, and coverage.

2.6 Recording Fees

- Property Deed Recording: A charge for recording the new property deed with the neighborhood authorities, commonly ranging from $50 to $one hundred fifty.

3. Common Closing Costs for Sellers

3.1 Real Estate Agent Commission

- Commission Fees: The rate paid to actual property marketers for their services in promoting the belongings. This is generally a percentage of the sale charge, regularly round 5% to six%, and is normally cut up between the purchaser's and supplier's agents.

3.2 Title and Transfer Fees

- Title Insurance: Seller may be accountable for offering a title insurance policy for the client.
- Transfer Tax: Some jurisdictions impose a tax at the transfer of property ownership, which could range based on the sale fee and region. This price is on occasion negotiable between buyer and supplier.

3.3 Mortgage Payoff Costs

- Payoff Statement Fee: A charge for obtaining a assertion from the lender detailing the exact quantity needed to pay off the present loan.

Prepayment Penalty: Some mortgages have a prepayment penalty if the loan is paid off early. This price is much less common however can be sizable.

4. How to Budget for Closing Costs

4.1 Estimate Costs in Advance

- Use a Closing Cost Calculator: Online calculators can offer a difficult estimate of remaining charges based on the property's buy charge and place.
- Request a Good Faith Estimate (GFE): Lenders are required to offer a GFE, which outlines the expected final costs and fees, usually furnished early inside the mortgage utility procedure.

4.2 Plan for Additional Costs

Contingency Fund: Set apart additional finances to cowl any unexpected fees that can get up all through the final manner. A true rule of thumb is to budget an extra 1% to a few% of the purchase fee for unforeseen fees.

4.3 Review the Closing Disclosure

Closing Disclosure Form: A distinct assertion supplied by way of the lender at the least three days before closing that outlines the final last expenses and loan phrases. Review this file carefully to make sure all prices align with preceding estimates and to cope with any discrepancies.

CHAPTER 4: FINDING AND EVALUATING PROPERTIES

PROPERTY SEARCH STRATEGIES
DUE DILIGENCE IN REAL ESTATE INVESTING

1. Introduction to Due Diligence
- Definition: Due diligence in actual estate making an investment includes very well investigating and evaluating a belongings earlier than finishing a transaction. This method guarantees that the investment aligns together with your dreams, meets legal requirements, and is loose from hidden dangers or troubles.
- Importance: Performing due diligence enables pick out capability troubles, validate the belonging's cost, and mitigate dangers, making sure that the investment is sound and that there aren't any surprising surprises after buy.

2. Key Areas of Due Diligence

2.1 Property Inspection

- Home Inspection: Hire a expert inspector to assess the asset's situation, inclusive of structural factors, systems (plumbing, electrical, HVAC), and standard protection. Look for issues along with water harm, foundation troubles, or outdated structures.
- Specialized Inspections: Depending at the belongings, additional inspections may be essential, including pest inspections, mildew inspections, or radon checking out.

2.2 Financial Analysis

- Comparative Market Analysis (CMA): Evaluate latest sales of comparable residences inside the place to decide if the acquisition fee is cheap and aggressive.

- Income and Expense Analysis: For condominium properties, review ancient profits and rate information to evaluate the property's profitability. Analyze hire rolls, running expenses, and any potential for future income boom.
- Investment Return Calculations: Calculate key metrics inclusive of cash glide, cap charge (capitalization fee), and go back on investment (ROI) to assess the property's financial performance.

2.3 Legal and Title Review

- Title Search: Conduct a title search to ensure there aren't any liens, encumbrances, or legal claims against the property. Title insurance can defend against destiny claims.
- Deed Verification: Verify that the vendor has clear ownership of the assets

and the right to sell it. Review the deed for any regulations or covenants.

Zoning and Land Use: Check local zoning laws and land use rules to make certain the property can be used as supposed and that there are no restrictions affecting your plans.

2.4 Property Documentation

- Property Disclosure Statement: Review the vendor's disclosure declaration, which affords facts about the property's situation and any acknowledged problems.

- Lease Agreements: For apartment properties, take a look at current hire agreements to recognize tenant rights, lease phrases, and rental profits.

2.5 Environmental and Structural Concerns

- Environmental Assessments: Conduct an environmental web page evaluation to identify potential infection or environmental risks on the property, particularly for business properties.

Structural Analysis: If relevant, check the situation of the asset's basis, roof, and other structural factors to pick out any potential problems or required upkeep.

2.6 Market and Neighborhood Analysis

- Neighborhood Research: Investigate the nearby neighborhood to evaluate factors inclusive of crime quotes, faculty great, and overall desirability. Look for symptoms of neighborhood improvement or decline.
- Market Trends: Analyze nearby real property market trends, which include belongings values, condo prices, and emptiness fees, to recognize the area's monetary and real estate fitness.

3. Steps in the Due Diligence Process

3.1 Preliminary Research

- Initial Property Review: Conduct initial studies on the belongings, which includes a primary online search, reviewing available list statistics, and assessing the general situation and neighborhood.
- Engage Professionals: Hire certified professionals, including real estate agents, inspectors, appraisers, and lawyers, to help inside the due diligence procedure.

3.2 Contract Contingencies

- Include Contingencies: Negotiate settlement contingencies to allow for due diligence investigations. Common contingencies consist of inspection contingencies, financing contingencies, and appraisal contingencies.

- Review Contract Terms: Carefully evaluate the acquisition settlement to recognize the phrases, situations, and closing dates associated with due diligence.

3.3 Documentation Review

- Obtain and Review Documents: Collect all relevant files related to the property, which includes inspection reports, monetary records, and legal documents. Review these files very well to perceive any issues or concerns.
- Address Issues: If any issues or discrepancies are discovered in the course of due diligence, cope with them with the seller. Negotiate maintenance, rate modifications, or different treatments as wanted.

3.4 Final Decision

Evaluate Findings: Assess all due diligence findings to determine if the belongings meets your funding criteria and if the ability blessings outweigh the dangers.

Make an Informed Decision: Decide whether to proceed with the acquisition, renegotiate terms, or walk far from the deal based totally on the consequences of your due diligence.

PROPERTY INSPECTIONS IN REAL ESTATE INVESTING

1. Introduction to Property Inspections

- Definition: Property inspections involve an in depth examination of a asset's situation to become aware of any potential troubles or vital repairs. Inspections are typically conducted by means of professional inspectors and are crucial for each customers and sellers to make certain transparency and knowledgeable selection making.
- Importance: Property inspections help uncover hidden issues that could have an

effect on the property's price, protection, or livability. They provide precious statistics for negotiating maintenance or adjustments in the purchase charge.

2. Types of Property Inspections

2.1 General Home Inspection

- Scope: A comprehensive inspection overlaying principal structures and additives of the assets, together with the inspiration, roof, plumbing, electric systems, HVAC (heating, ventilation, and air conditioning), and popular structural integrity.
- Purpose: To identify any visible defects or troubles that could have an effect on the belonging's price or require repair. It allows shoppers recognize the overall circumstance of the property.

2.2 Specialized Inspections

- Pest Inspection: Examines the property for signs of pest infestations, including termites, rodents, or different harmful insects. This is especially crucial in regions prone to pest issues.

- Mold Inspection: Identifies mildew boom and capacity moisture issues that might have an effect on indoor air satisfactory and health. Mold inspections frequently encompass checking out air samples and assessing hidden mold resources.

- Radon Testing: Measures radon gasoline levels in the property. Radon is a colorless, odorless gas which can pose health dangers if present in excessive concentrations.

- Asbestos Inspection: Checks for the presence of asbestos containing substances, specifically in older homes. Asbestos can pose health risks if disturbed or deteriorating.

2.3 Commercial Property Inspections

- Scope: Includes comparable additives as residential inspections however tailored to commercial houses, such as office buildings, retail spaces, or business centers. Focuses on structural integrity, HVAC structures, electric and plumbing systems, and compliance with business building codes.
- Purpose: To assess the situation and functionality of industrial property components and become aware of any troubles that might affect the property's usability or profitability.

3. Steps in the Property Inspection Process

3.1 Pre Inspection Preparation

- Select a Qualified Inspector: Choose a licensed and experienced inspector with an awesome popularity.

Recommendations from actual property dealers or other investors can be useful.

Schedule the Inspection: Arrange the inspection in advance and make sure the property is obtainable. Coordinate with the vendor or the vendor's agent to confirm the date and time.

3.2 Conducting the Inspection

- On Site Examination: The inspector will go to the property to carry out a thorough examination, checking various systems, systems, and additives for issues or symptoms of damage.
- Documentation: The inspector will report their findings via notes, images, and probably video. They will examine the severity of issues and their ability impact at the belongings.

3.3 Review of Inspection Report

- Receive the Report: After the inspection, the inspector will provide a detailed file outlining their findings. This record will include descriptions of any troubles, their severity, and pointers for repair or in addition assessment.

- Analyze Findings: Review the record cautiously to recognize the condition of the property. Pay attention to fundamental issues, consisting of structural troubles or enormous protection hazards.

3.Four Negotiation and Decision Making

- Address Issues with the Seller: Use the inspection document to barter maintenance, rate reductions, or other adjustments with the vendor. Focus on important troubles that might affect the belonging's value or require tremendous funding.

- Decide on Next Steps: Based on the inspection findings and negotiations, decide whether or not to continue with the purchase, request repairs, or withdraw from the transaction.

4. Cost of Property Inspections

4.1 Residential Inspections

- Typical Costs: Home inspection expenses commonly variety from $300 to $six hundred, relying at the assets size, region, and complexity. Specialized inspections, inclusive of pest or mildew inspections, might also incur extra expenses.

4.2 Commercial Inspections

- Typical Costs: Commercial belongings inspections may be extra steeply priced, often ranging from $1,000 to $5,000 or greater, depending on the property size, type, and specific necessities.

MARKET COMPARISONS IN REAL ESTATE INVESTING

1. Introduction to Market Comparisons

- Definition: Market comparisons involve analyzing and comparing comparable residences in a given area to evaluate a property's price, market tendencies, and investment capacity. This method enables buyers make informed selections through offering context and benchmarks for pricing and overall performance.

Importance: Accurate market comparisons are vital for figuring out honest assets cost, setting aggressive pricing, and know how neighborhood market conditions.

2. Types of Market Comparisons

2.1 Comparative Market Analysis (CMA)

Purpose: A CMA evaluates these days offered properties similar to the one under consideration to estimate its honest marketplace fee. It considers elements like property size, place, age, and circumstance.

Components:

- Sold Comparables: Properties which have offered recently and are similar in functions and region. These provide a baseline for estimating the property's fee.
- Active Listings: Currently indexed residences which can be much like the belongings in query. These help gauge contemporary market opposition and pricing.
- Expired Listings: Properties that were listed but did now not promote. Analyzing those can monitor pricing problems or market challenges.

2.2 Rent Comparisons

- Purpose: Rent comparisons analyze apartment costs of comparable residences to determine capability rental profits and determine the property's beauty as a condominium investment.

Components:

Comparable Rentals: Recently rented homes similar in size, location, and amenities. This offers a benchmark for putting competitive condo charges.

Vacancy Rates: Current vacancy costs in the location can imply rental demand and assist investigate the property's condominium ability.

2.3 Investment Comparisons

Purpose: Evaluates investment properties based totally on metrics inclusive of coins flow, cap rate, and ROI to determine the attractiveness and performance of various homes.

Components:
- Cash Flow Analysis: Compares internet income from homes after expenses to evaluate profitability.
- Cap Rate (Capitalization Rate): A measure of the assets's go back on funding, calculated by using dividing the

once a year internet working income by using the property's purchase rate.

ROI (Return on Investment): Compares the investment's profitability with the aid of dividing net profit via the overall investment price.

3. Steps in Conducting Market Comparisons

3.1 Define Property Parameters

- Identify Key Features: Determine the critical traits of the property, such as kind (residential, business), length, area, age, and situation.
- Set Comparison Criteria: Establish the criteria for choosing comparable homes, making sure they are similar in key aspects.

3.2 Collect Data

Gather Market Data: Obtain facts on currently bought properties, cutting edge listings, and apartment quotes from real property databases, MLS (Multiple Listing

Service), or neighborhood actual estate dealers.

Analyze Trends: Review historical market trends, which includes assets cost adjustments, condo charge fluctuations, and nearby financial situations.

3.3 Analyze Comparables

- Evaluate Comparables: Compare the chosen houses in opposition to the subject property. Assess variations in functions, situations, and pricing.
- Adjust for Differences: Make changes to account for variations among the difficulty property and comparables, together with size, situation, or area.

3.4 Assess Market Conditions

- Current Market Trends: Analyze broader marketplace tendencies, such as deliver and demand, economic indicators, and nearby actual property situations.

- Local Factors: Consider factors like community development, infrastructure initiatives, and demographic changes that could effect belongings values.

3.5 Determine Value and Performance

- Estimate Property Value: Based on the analysis, estimate the truthful marketplace value of the belongings.
- Evaluate Investment Potential: Assess the investment capability by means of evaluating projected returns, coins glide, and overall performance metrics with other similar houses.

4. Tools for Market Comparisons

4.1 Real Estate Databases

- MLS: Multiple Listing Service provides comprehensive statistics on assets sales, listings, and marketplace trends.
- Real Estate Websites: Platforms like Zillow, Realtor.Com, and Redfin offer

property information, comparables, and marketplace insights.

4.2 Analysis Software

- Comparative Analysis Tools: Software and apps designed for actual estate experts to carry out designated marketplace comparisons and valuation analyses.
- Spreadsheet Tools: Excel or Google Sheets may be used to arrange and analyze marketplace facts and perform monetary calculations.

CHAPTER 5: MANAGING YOUR INVESTMENTS

PROPERTY MANAGEMENT

SELF MANAGEMENT VS. HIRING A PROPERTY MANAGER

1. Introduction
- Definition: Self control entails coping with all components of belongings management in my view, whilst hiring a property supervisor way entrusting a expert with those obligations.
- Importance: Deciding among self management and hiring a belongings manager impacts the efficiency, profitability, and personal involvement in managing rental homes.

2. Self Management

2.1 Advantages

- Cost Savings: Avoid management costs, which generally range from 8% to 12% of the monthly hire. This may be significant if you have multiple homes or excessive condominium earnings.
- Direct Control: Full manipulate over each aspect of property control, such as tenant selection, preservation choices, and financial control. This permits for a extra finger son technique and instantaneous decision making.
- Personal Touch: Opportunity to build nonpublic relationships with tenants, that may beautify tenant pleasure and retention.

2.2 Disadvantages

- Time Commitment: Requires a giant time funding for obligations along with tenant verbal exchange, maintenance, and rent series. This can be challenging when you have multiple homes or a annoying agenda.

- Expertise Needed: Requires knowledge of property control laws, upkeep techniques, and tenant members of the family. Lack of expertise can cause mistakes or legal problems.
- Emergency Handling: Responsibility for coping with emergencies, upkeep, and tenant court cases 24/7, which can be stressful and disruptive.

2.3 Key Responsibilities

- Tenant Screening: Conduct historical past assessments, confirm condo history, and make certain tenant qualifications.
- Rent Collection: Collect lease payments, handle overdue costs, and control monetary facts.
- Maintenance and Repairs: Address preservation requests, agenda upkeep,

and manage contractors or service carriers.

Legal Compliance: Ensure adherence to nearby, nation, and federal guidelines, including truthful housing legal guidelines and eviction processes.

3. Hiring a Property Manager

3.1 Advantages

- Professional Expertise: Property managers have enjoy and knowledge in managing property control duties, prison necessities, and tenant family members. They can navigate complicated issues greater successfully.
- Time Savings: Offloads management obligations, freeing up time for other sports or investments. This is in particular useful if you personal more than one homes or produce other commitments.

- Streamlined Operations: Property managers handle all factors of assets management, inclusive of advertising, tenant screening, protection, and monetary management, leading to greater efficient operations.

3.2 Disadvantages

- Management Fees: Property management organizations typically rate prices ranging from 8% to twelve% of the month to month hire, plus additional fees for offerings including leasing, maintenance, or inspections.
- Less Control: Limited direct involvement in everyday management decisions. This might also result in much less personalized carrier or specific control styles than you will in my opinion put into effect.
- Potential for Miscommunication: Misunderstandings or

miscommunications among you and the property manager can arise, which may additionally affect tenant delight or assets protection.

3.3 Key Responsibilities of a Property Manager

- Tenant Acquisition: Market the property, show it to prospective tenants, and cope with rent agreements and passins.
- Rent Collection: Collect hire, handle past due bills, and manipulate economic statistics.
- Maintenance and Repairs: Coordinate and oversee upkeep and repairs, such as emergency troubles.
- Legal Compliance: Ensure compliance with all relevant laws and rules, cope with evictions, and manipulate tenant disputes.

4. Factors to Consider When Deciding

4.1 Property Type and Location

- Complexity: Higher complexity or a couple of properties may benefit from expert management due to the scale and varied needs.
- Location: Properties in one of a kind locations would possibly require special stages of neighborhood marketplace understanding, which a assets supervisor can offer.

4.2 Personal Time and Expertise

- Time Availability: Assess your potential to manage the assets correctly given your other commitments.
- Expertise: Consider your knowledge of property control, nearby laws, and maintenance.

4.3 Financial Goals

- Cost vs. Benefit: Evaluate whether the capacity cost savings from self management outweigh the blessings of hiring a assets supervisor, such as time financial savings and professional expertise.

MAINTENANCE AND REPAIRS IN REAL ESTATE INVESTING

1. Introduction

- Definition: Maintenance and upkeep involve the continued care and solving of issues inside a belongings to ensure it stays in true circumstance, useful, and attractive. Effective control of those obligations is vital for retaining assets value and tenant pleasure.

- Importance: Regular maintenance and prompt upkeep assist save you high priced problems, make bigger the lifespan of property additives, and make a contribution to a fantastic apartment enjoy.

2. Types of Maintenance and Repairs

2.1 Routine Maintenance

- Definition: Regular, scheduled obligations aimed toward stopping wear and tear and maintaining the property in most suitable circumstance.

Examples:

- HVAC System Maintenance: Changing filters, cleaning ducts, and servicing heating and cooling systems.
- Plumbing Checks: Inspecting for leaks, cleansing drains, and ensuring water warmers are functioning nicely.
- Roof and Gutter Maintenance: Cleaning gutters, checking for damage, and analyzing roof shingles.
- Landscaping: Regular backyard paintings, together with mowing, trimming, and handling garden beds.

2.2 Preventive Maintenance

Definition: Actions taken to prevent capability issues earlier than they arise, often based totally on producer pointers or industry excellent practices.

Examples:
- Pest Control: Regular remedies or inspections to prevent infestations.
- Sealant Application: Applying sealants to driveways, decks, or windows to shield in opposition to weather harm.
- Siding and Exterior Maintenance: Inspecting and repairing siding to prevent water harm and mildew boom.

2.Three Emergency Repairs

Definition: Unplanned upkeep had to cope with urgent problems that might have an effect on the safety or habitability of the belongings.

Examples:

- Plumbing Emergencies: Fixing burst pipes, sewer backups, or principal leaks.
- Electrical Issues: Addressing power outages, faulty wiring, or electric hazards.
- Structural Damage: Repairing harm from storms, injuries, or foundation issues.

2.4 Cosmetic Repairs

Definition: Repairs geared toward enhancing the appearance of the assets with out addressing practical problems.

Examples:
- Painting: Repainting walls, ceilings, or exteriors to refresh the appearance of the belongings.
- Flooring: Repairing or changing broken flooring, such as carpets or tiles.
- Fixtures: Updating or repairing furniture like taps, light furniture, or cabinetry.

3. Managing Maintenance and Repairs

3.1 Planning and Scheduling

- Create a Maintenance Schedule: Develop a calendar for ordinary and preventive renovation tasks to make certain they're completed regularly and on time.
- Budget for Maintenance: Allocate price range for your finances for both ordinary and sudden upkeep to keep away from monetary pressure when troubles arise.

3.2 Hiring Professionals

- Find Qualified Contractors: Research and hire licensed and experienced specialists for specialized obligations, such as HVAC technicians, plumbers, or electricians.
- Get Multiple Quotes: Obtain quotes from numerous contractors to examine expenses and offerings before

committing to a restore or maintenance task.

Check References and Reviews: Verify the contractor's popularity through references, critiques, and any available credentials.

3.3 Handling Tenant Requests

- Respond Promptly: Address preservation requests and repair troubles from tenants as quickly as feasible to hold tenant pride and prevent in addition harm.

- Communicate Clearly: Keep tenants informed about the status in their requests, inclusive of timelines for maintenance and any essential preparations.

3.4 Documenting Work

- Record Maintenance and Repairs: Maintain certain facts of all maintenance and restore sports, which includes dates, prices, and outlines of labor accomplished.

Keep Receipts and Invoices: Store all receipts and invoices related to protection and maintenance for accounting and tax purposes.

4. Cost Management

4.1 Budgeting for Repairs

- Estimate Costs: Use historic statistics and market research to estimate the fees of ordinary and ability emergency upkeep.
- Create a Contingency Fund: Set apart a contingency fund for surprising repairs and emergencies. A not unusual recommendation is to finances 1% to a few% of the belonging's price yearly for preservation and repairs.

4.2 Cost Saving Strategies

- Perform Regular Inspections: Identify and cope with minor problems earlier than they end up foremost troubles, which can help shop money on maintenance.

- DIY Maintenance: Handle easy upkeep tasks your self, along with converting air filters or cleansing gutters, to reduce charges.
- Negotiate with Contractors: Seek reductions or negotiate pricing for bulk work or ongoing relationships with contractors.

TENANT RELATIONS IN REAL ESTATE INVESTING

1. Introduction

- Definition: Tenant relations contain dealing with and keeping interactions between landlords or belongings managers and tenants. Positive tenant family members are crucial for making sure tenant pride, retention, and a easy operation of condo residences.

- Importance: Effective tenant family members assist lessen turnover, save you disputes, and enhance the overall enjoy for both landlords and tenants.

2. Key Aspects of Tenant Relations

2.1 Communication

- Clear and Open Communication: Maintain transparent and powerful communique channels with tenants. Ensure that tenants have a clean expertise of belongings policies, rent phrases, and expectations.
- Regular Updates: Keep tenants informed about vital statistics such as protection schedules, changes in assets control, or updates in rules.
- Responsive Service: Respond right away to tenant inquiries, maintenance requests, or lawsuits. Timely and courteous responses construct trust and display reliability.

2.2 Lease Agreements

- Detailed Agreements: Ensure lease agreements are comprehensive, detailing phrases along with lease quantity, payment due dates, hire duration, and duties for renovation.
- Legal Compliance: Regularly overview and replace hire agreements to conform with neighborhood, country, and federal regulations. Include clauses that guard each parties and cope with capacity problems.

2.3 Maintenance and Repairs

- Timely Maintenance: Address preservation requests and upkeep right away to ensure the belongings stays in good circumstance and to keep tenants glad.
- Routine Maintenance: Implement a time table for everyday upkeep responsibilities, such as HVAC servicing,

plumbing checks, and landscaping, to prevent large issues and hold belongings fee.

2.4 Conflict Resolution

- Address Issues Early: Handle conflicts or problems between tenants or among tenants and the landlord swiftly to prevent escalation.

- Fair and Objective: Approach disputes impartially and are looking for to recognize all perspectives before making decisions. Document all interactions and resolutions to provide clarity and help if needed.

2.5 Tenant Retention

- Provide Good Service: Ensure that tenants have a high quality residing experience by retaining the assets properly, being aware of requests, and imparting a clean, safe surroundings.

- Incentives for Renewal: Offer incentives consisting of renewal discounts, upgrades, or minor improvements to inspire tenants to renew their leases.
- Build Relationships: Foster properly relationships by way of showing appreciation for tenants and tasty with them positively.

2.6 Rent Collection and Financial Management

- Efficient Rent Collection: Implement a reliable device for accumulating lease, whether online or via different secure techniques. Clearly speak payment due dates and techniques.
- Late Payment Policies: Establish clean policies for coping with late bills, consisting of late expenses and processes for addressing persistent non price problems.

3. Tools and Strategies for Effective Tenant Relations

3.1 Property Management Software

- Features: Use property control software program to streamline verbal exchange, control renovation requests, track hire bills, and preserve statistics. Many systems provide tenant portals for smooth get right of entry to to facts and services.

- Benefits: Improves efficiency, reduces administrative burdens, and enhances tenant revel in by supplying smooth get admission to to belongings associated facts and offerings.

3.2 Tenant Surveys

- Feedback Collection: Conduct surveys to collect feedback from tenants approximately their reviews and identify regions for development.

Actionable Insights: Use survey outcomes to deal with worries, make upgrades, and enhance tenant delight.

3.3 Education and Resources

- Tenant Handbook: Provide tenants with a handbook or guide outlining assets regulations, protection processes, and make contact with records. This facilitates set clean expectations and provides a reference for tenants.
- Regular Updates: Share educational sources or updates on subjects along with preservation guidelines, network events, or local services.

FINANCIAL MANAGEMENT IN REAL ESTATE INVESTING

1. Introduction

Definition: Financial control in real estate investing involves overseeing and controlling the financial factors of property investments, which includes budgeting, accounting, cash go with the flow control, and monetary making plans. Effective financial management is vital for maximizing profitability and making sure long term fulfillment.

Importance: Proper monetary management enables buyers make knowledgeable decisions, preserve profitability, and manage risks related to actual estate investments.

2. Key Components of Financial Management

2.1 Budgeting

Create a Budget: Develop a complete price range that includes all predicted earnings and prices related to the belongings. This have to cowl mortgage payments, assets taxes, coverage, preservation, and management costs.

- Track Expenses: Regularly screen and file all charges to make sure they align with the price range. This allows discover regions where fees can be controlled or reduced.

- Adjust as Needed: Review and alter the price range periodically to mirror adjustments in profits, fees, or funding techniques.

2.2 Accounting and Record Keeping

- Maintain Financial Records: Keep correct and precise information of all economic transactions, consisting of lease payments, fees, repairs, and different charges. This is essential for tax reporting and monetary evaluation.

- Use Accounting Software: Employ accounting software program or assets control systems to streamline document retaining, track transactions, and generate financial reports.

- Reconcile Accounts: Regularly reconcile bank statements together with your statistics to make certain accuracy and pick out discrepancies.

2.3 Cash Flow Management

- Monitor Cash Flow: Track the float of coins into and out of the assets to make certain sufficient budget for operating costs, loan payments, and sudden costs.
- Optimize Cash Flow: Implement techniques to decorate coins float, along with growing rent, decreasing costs, or managing emptiness fees.
- Create a Reserve Fund: Maintain a reserve fund for emergencies and sudden upkeep to avoid monetary pressure.

2.4 Financial Analysis

- Evaluate Property Performance: Analyze economic metrics which includes Net Operating Income (NOI), Cap Rate (Capitalization Rate), and Return on Investment (ROI) to assess the performance of your home.

- Compare Properties: Use economic evaluation to evaluate distinctive funding residences and determine their relative profitability and risk.
- Review Investment Goals: Regularly check your funding dreams and overall performance metrics to ensure alignment together with your basic approach.

2.5 Tax Management

- Understand Tax Implications: Familiarize yourself with tax laws and rules associated with actual property investments, which includes deductions, depreciation, and capital gains.
- Maximize Deductions: Take benefit of to be had tax deductions, along with loan interest, belongings taxes, and restore costs, to lessen taxable earnings.

Consult a Tax Professional: Work with a tax marketing consultant or accountant who specializes in actual estate to optimize your tax approach and make certain compliance.

2.6 Financing and Mortgage Management

- Select Financing Options: Choose appropriate financing alternatives for your private home, such as conventional loans, nonpublic lenders, or crowdfunding. Evaluate hobby fees, terms, and compensation plans.
- Manage Mortgage Payments: Keep song of loan bills and make sure they're made on time to keep away from penalties or damage in your credit score score.
- Refinance if Beneficial: Consider refinancing alternatives in the event that they offer better phrases or lower hobby quotes which can improve coins drift and universal profitability.

3. Financial Reporting

3.1 Regular Reports

- Generate Reports: Create regular economic reports that summarize earnings, costs, and coins waft. These reports offer insights into the asset's monetary performance and help in decision making.

- Review Reports: Analyze economic reviews to become aware of developments, determine performance, and make knowledgeable selections approximately property control and investment strategies.

3.2 Performance Metrics

Net Operating Income (NOI): Calculate NOI by way of subtracting operating prices from gross condominium earnings. This metric assesses the belonging's profitability before financing costs.

- Cap Rate (Capitalization Rate): Determine the Cap Rate with the aid of dividing NOI by the property's purchase charge. This metric helps examine the assets's go back on funding.
- Return on Investment (ROI): Calculate ROI via dividing the belonging's internet income by way of the total funding cost. This metric measures the general go back at the investment.

RENT COLLECTION IN REAL ESTATE INVESTING

1. Introduction
- Definition: Rent collection refers back to the procedure of receiving and handling apartment payments from tenants.
- Importance: Efficient rent series practices help make certain well timed

bills, reduce overdue prices, and hold a nice relationship with tenants.

2. Key Aspects of Rent Collection

2.1 Setting Up a System

- Payment Methods: Offer a couple of price alternatives to house tenants' options. Common strategies encompass on line payments, direct bank transfers, assessments, and charge apps.
- Online Payment Platforms: Utilize assets management software program or on line fee systems that streamline lease collection and provide tenants with a convenient way to pay electronically.
- Automated Payments: Set up automated fee reminders and recurring bills to lessen the likelihood of past due bills.

2.2 Communication and Expectations

- Clear Terms: Clearly define rent fee terms in the rent settlement, such as the

due date, everyday fee techniques, and any past due expenses.
- Regular Reminders: Send reminders earlier than the rent due date to make sure tenants are aware of upcoming payments. Use email, textual content messages, or computerized notifications.
- Late Payment Policy: Clearly talk the effects of past due payments, such as any relevant overdue fees and the manner for addressing past due bills.

2.3 Handling Payments
- Record Transactions: Maintain accurate information of all lease payments, such as dates, quantities, and fee methods. This helps tune payments and manipulate financial statistics.
- Deposit Checks Promptly: If accepting assessments, deposit them promptly to avoid delays and make sure budget are to be had in your account.

Verify Payments: Confirm receipt of bills and deal with any discrepancies or issues directly to maintain correct records and solve tenant worries.

2.4 Addressing Late Payments

- Late Fees: Implement a fair and transparent past due rate coverage, as outlined within the rent agreement. Ensure charges are reasonable and observe nearby regulations.
- Grace Period: Consider imparting a grace duration before assessing overdue fees to provide tenants with a buffer in case of monetary problems or unexpected circumstances.
- Collections Process: Develop a clear procedure for dealing with overdue bills, including sending reminders, issuing formal notices, and potentially beginning felony action if necessary.

2.5 Handling Non Payment

- Communication: Reach out to tenants who fail to pay on time to recognize the reason for non charge and explore possible answers or price preparations.

- Payment Plans: Consider imparting price plans or temporary comfort options for tenants going through monetary problems. Ensure agreements are documented and enforceable.

- Eviction Process: If non fee persists, comply with the legal eviction procedure in your region. Ensure all steps are dealt with in step with nearby laws and policies to avoid felony headaches.

3. Best Practices

3.1 Tenant Screening

PreRental Screening: Conduct thorough tenant screening to assess monetary balance and condominium history. This can assist lessen the chance of nonpayment and make sure reliable tenants.

3.2 Financial Management

- Budgeting: Include hire series on your budgeting and monetary making plans to make sure you have got sufficient budget for property charges and investments.
- Cash Flow Monitoring: Regularly monitor coins float to perceive and address any problems related to lease collection and make sure timely bills.

3.3 Legal Compliance

- Local Laws: Familiarize yourself with neighborhood legal guidelines and rules related to rent series, overdue prices, and eviction procedures to make certain compliance.
- Lease Agreements: Ensure lease agreements honestly outline price terms, late prices, and the technique for

managing non fee to protect your rights and enforce ability.

EXPENSE TRACKING IN REAL ESTATE INVESTING

1. Introduction

- Definition: Expense monitoring entails recording and tracking all fees related to belongings management and investment. This includes costs related to retaining, running, and improving condominium properties.
- Importance: Accurate expense monitoring is critical for dealing with coins go with the flow, budgeting efficaciously, maximizing profitability, and ensuring financial transparency.

2. Key Components of Expense Tracking

2.1 Categories of Expenses

Operating Expenses: Regular costs incurred in the day today control of the belongings, inclusive of utilities, belongings control fees, and insurance.

- Maintenance and Repairs: Costs associated with retaining and repairing the belongings, along with ordinary preservation, emergency maintenance, and contractor services.
- Capital Expenditures: Large, onetime investments in property upgrades or improvements, such as transforming, roof replacements, or main systems upgrades.
- Property Taxes: Taxes levied at the belongings, that may range primarily based on vicinity and belongings cost.
- Mortgage Payments: Payments toward the belonging's loan, such as essential and interest.

2.2 Tracking Methods

- Manual Records: Use spreadsheets or ledgers to manually document fees. This

technique can be effective for small portfolios however may additionally come to be bulky because the wide variety of houses will increase.
- Accounting Software: Utilize accounting software or assets management systems to automate fee tracking. These gear frequently provide features which include expense categorization, reporting, and integration with financial institution accounts.
- Expense Management Apps: Employ cell apps designed for price tracking to capture and categorize expenses on the pass, such as receipt scanning and actual time cost entry.

2.Three Recording Expenses
- Document Receipts: Keep physical or virtual copies of all receipts and invoices associated with belongings costs. This facilitates make certain accuracy and

gives proof for accounting and tax functions.

- Enter Expenses Promptly: Record expenses as quickly as they occur to keep away from lacking or forgetting transactions. Regular updates prevent backlog and make sure correct monetary facts.
- Categorize Expenses: Assign fees to appropriate classes to facilitate special economic evaluation and reporting. Consistent categorization aids in budgeting and tax practise.

2.4 Monitoring and Analyzing Expenses

- Review Regularly: Periodically evaluate fee reports to reveal spending styles, pick out areas for value savings, and make certain costs align with the finances.
- Analyze Trends: Analyze fee developments over the years to assess

the effect of various prices on average profitability. Look for styles that might imply areas for improvement or performance.

Compare with Budget: Compare actual fees to budgeted amounts to become aware of deviations and regulate the finances or spending as needed.

2.5 Tax Considerations

- Deductible Expenses: Identify which costs are tax deductible and make certain they may be nicely recorded. Common deductible charges include property management expenses, preservation prices, and mortgage hobby.

- Organize Documentation: Keep organized information of all deductible expenses to help tax filings and audits. Use accounting software to generate tax reports and simplify the tax practise procedure.

3. Best Practices

3.1 Consistency

- Standardize Procedures: Implement steady strategies for recording and categorizing expenses to preserve accuracy and simplicity of tracking.
- Regular Updates: Update price facts regularly to make certain well timed and accurate economic records.

TAX DEDUCTIONS IN REAL ESTATE INVESTING

1. Introduction

Definition: Tax deductions are charges that may be subtracted from a assets investor's gross profits to lessen taxable profits and, consequently, the amount of tax owed. Understanding and maximizing tax deductions is crucial for optimizing monetary performance and decreasing tax liability.

Importance: Properly utilizing tax deductions can drastically effect profitability and coins glide, making it a critical thing of financial management for real estate investors.

2. Common Tax Deductions for Real Estate Investors

2.1 Mortgage Interest

- Description: Interest paid on a loan for a rental property is deductible. This includes hobby on loans used to accumulate or enhance the assets.
- Documentation: Keep data of loan hobby payments, generally furnished in a Form 1098 with the aid of the lender.

2.2 Property Taxes

- Description: Property taxes paid to neighborhood governments are deductible. This consists of taxes assessed at the real property belongings itself.

Documentation: Retain copies of property tax payments and proof of charge.

2.3 Depreciation

- Description: Depreciation lets in you to deduct the fee of the belongings over a period of time. For residential homes, the standard depreciation duration is 27.5 years, even as for business houses, it's far 39 years.

- Documentation: Maintain precise records of property acquisition fees and enhancements. Depreciation is commonly calculated the usage of IRS hints.

2.4 Repairs and Maintenance

- Description: Costs for upkeep and preservation that hold the assets in desirable situation are deductible. This consists of fees for fixing leaks, portray, or replacing damaged fixtures.

Documentation: Keep receipts and statistics of all repair and maintenance sports.

2.5 Utilities

- Description: If you pay for utilities (which include water, energy, or gasoline) on behalf of your tenants, these costs are deductible. If tenants pay utilities immediately, those are not deductible.
- Documentation: Retain utility bills and information of payment.

2.6 Property Management Fees

- Description: Fees paid to assets management corporations for handling condo houses are deductible. This consists of costs for handling tenant issues, accumulating rent, and maintaining the property.
- Documentation: Keep invoices and statistics of payments to assets control organizations.

2.7 Insurance Premiums

- Description: Premiums for insurance policies associated with the condominium belongings, which include danger insurance and liability insurance, are deductible.

- Documentation: Retain copies of coverage regulations and proof of charge.

2.8 Legal and Professional Fees

- Description: Fees paid to legal professionals, accountants, or different specialists for services associated with the assets, along with felony recommendation, tax preparation, or actual estate consulting, are deductible.

- Documentation: Keep invoices and records of professional offerings rendered.

2.9 Travel Expenses

Description: If you travel for assets management functions or to visit multiple condo properties, you may be able to deduct journey charges consisting of mileage, lodging, and food.

Documentation: Maintain statistics of journey fees, which includes mileage logs, receipts, and itineraries.

2.10 Advertising Costs

Description: Costs for marketing condo residences, which includes online listings, newspaper ads, or signage, are deductible.

Documentation: Keep copies of classified ads and invoices for advertising services.

3. Best Practices for Maximizing Tax Deductions

3.1 Maintain Accurate Records

- Documentation: Keep thorough and prepared facts of all charges associated with the belongings. This includes receipts, invoices, financial institution statements, and contracts.

Record Keeping System: Use accounting software program or spreadsheets to music prices and prepare documentation.

3.2 Consult a Tax Professional

- Expert Advice: Work with a tax advisor or accountant who specializes in actual estate to make certain you're maximizing deductions and complying with tax laws.
- Tax Planning: Seek recommendation on tax planning strategies, which include depreciation methods and capability deductions for improvements.

3.3 Stay Informed

- Tax Laws: Stay updated on modifications to tax legal guidelines and regulations that can impact your deductions. The IRS and neighborhood tax government may additionally replace guidelines and guidelines periodically.

www.ingramcontent.com/pod-product-compliance
Lightning Source LLC
Chambersburg PA
CBHW071921210526
45479CB00002B/509